Equal Access
Fighting for Disability Prot

D1363861

ADA and Your Rights at School and Work

Kerry Elizabeth Benson

Rosen
YA
New York

Published in 2020 by The Rosen Publishing Group, Inc.
29 East 21st Street, New York, NY 10010

Copyright © 2020 by The Rosen Publishing Group, Inc.

First Edition

All rights reserved. No part of this book may be reproduced in any form without permission in writing from the publisher, except by a reviewer.

Library of Congress Cataloging-in-Publication Data

Names: Benson, Kerry Elizabeth, author.
Title: ADA and your rights at school and work / Kerry Elizabeth Benson.
Other titles: Americans with Disabilities Act and your rights at school and work
Description: New York : Rosen Publishing Group, 2020 | Series: Equal access: fighting for disability protections | Includes bibliographical references and index.
Identifiers: LCCN 2018012933| ISBN 9781508183280 (library bound) | ISBN 9781508183273 (pbk.)
Subjects: LCSH: Teenagers with disabilities—Legal status, laws, etc.—United States—Juvenile literature. | Teenagers with disabilities—Education (Secondary)—United States—Juvenile literature. | Teenagers with disabilities—Vocational guidance—United States—Juvenile literature. | Teenagers with disabilities—Employment—United States—Juvenile literature. | United States. Americans with Disabilities Act of 1990—Juvenile literature. | Discrimination against people with disabilities—Law and legislation—United States—Juvenile literature.
Classification: LCC KF480 .B46 2020 | DDC 342.7308/7—dc23
LC record available at https://lccn.loc.gov/2018012933

Manufactured in the United States of America

The editors of this resource have consulted various organizations' style guides, including that of the National Center on Disability and Journalism, to ensure the language herein is accurate, sensitive, and respectful. In accordance with NCDJ's recommendation, we have deferred to our author's preference of either people-first or identity-first language.

For some of the images in this book, the people photographed are models and the depictions do not imply actual situations or events.

Contents

Introduction

Let's face it: growing up is hard. There are so many pressures that come along with being a teenager. But young people with disabilities often face even greater challenges. They may wonder how they will navigate a world that doesn't always seem like it was built for people like them. Maybe they have heard that there are laws protecting people with disabilities so that they can get the help that they need, but they are intimidated by legal terms, and they don't know where to start. Maybe they feel lost, overwhelmed, unsure of where to begin, and confused about how the law applies to them. They are not alone.

More than a million teenagers throughout the United States have disabilities. Many of these people live with invisible disabilities—those that aren't immediately apparent, like dyslexia, chronic pain, autism, or anxiety. Others, like wheelchair users and amputees, have more visible conditions. But whether their conditions are obvious or hidden, every one of them has the right to participate fully in society. They deserve the same opportunities as everybody else as they engage in education, employment, and leisure activities within the community.

The Americans with Disabilities Act (ADA) makes discrimination against individuals with disabilities illegal in all areas of public life. The law has been tremendously helpful in many ways, but many people with disabilities, especially young people,

Some people have visible disabilities, such as an amputation, while others have invisible disabilities that are difficult to recognize based on their appearance.

still face significant barriers. They might be discriminated against because of their disabilities, or maybe they deal with frequent accessibility issues in school, work, and the community—or both.

In an ideal world, the fact that the ADA exists would be enough to ensure equality for people with disabilities. Unfortunately, violations of the ADA are commonplace, and they often occur when business owners, school staff members, employers, and other community members are misinformed about the law. When people with disabilities are similarly misinformed, they may not realize that their rights have been violated. And even if they do suspect they aren't receiving the assistance or treatment they deserve under the ADA, they might not know where to turn for help or how to stand up for themselves.

By educating themselves about the ADA, teens with disabilities will learn how to speak up not only for themselves but also for every person with a disability. This guide will help young people with disabilities understand, use, and defend the rights that have been given to them by law so they can succeed in school, the workplace, and beyond.

Chapter One

Breaking Down the Law

Many people feel intimidated when they think about the legal system. Maybe they think of lawyers in fancy suits or heavy textbooks full of complicated terms that are beyond the understanding of the general public. But the law doesn't have to be scary and complicated. Laws are put in place to protect people, not to confuse them. The Americans with Disabilities Act (ADA) is a law that was established specifically to protect people with disabilities.

The Americans with Disabilities Act (ADA) was signed into law by President George H. W. Bush on July 26, 1990.

What Is the ADA?

The ADA says that people cannot be treated unfairly just because they have a disability. Its goal is to ensure that people with disabilities have the same opportunities as other people in school, work, transportation, and any other place that is available to the general public.

It may seem obvious that individuals with disabilities should have access to the same opportunities as everyone else, but the ADA didn't become a law

 The Five Titles

There are five different titles, or sections, of the ADA:

1. Employment (Title I): Title I requires that employers provide reasonable accommodations for applicants and employees who have disabilities. It also prohibits employers from discriminating against applicants and employees who have disabilities.

2. State and Local Government Activities (Title II): Title II prohibits state and local governments from discriminating against people with disabilities. Public transportation systems

like the Amtrak passenger railroad and city buses are covered under this section of the ADA.

3. Public Accommodations (Title III): Title III covers facilities such as hotels, grocery stores, restaurants, retail stores, and private transportation companies. This section of the ADA requires new construction and modifications to be accessible to people with disabilities, and it says that any features that make a public accommodation inaccessible must be removed if that removal would not prove too difficult.

4. Telecommunications (Title IV): Title IV requires telephone companies to provide services to people who are deaf/hard of hearing or who have speech difficulties so that these individuals can still communicate via telephone.

5. Miscellaneous (Title V): Title V covers issues that do not fit into the other four categories.

A woman uses sign language to make a phone call. Title IV of the ADA ensures that people with disabilities have equal access to telecommunication services.

until July 26, 1990. Eighteen years later, the ADA was updated with an amendment that expanded the definition of the word "disability" so that more people would be protected.

Whom Does the ADA Protect?

This teenager with a visual impairment is protected under the ADA because his condition greatly limits his ability to see his environment.

The ADA protects any person in the United States who has a disability. But what exactly does it mean to have a disability? The people in charge of writing this law wanted to make sure they answered that question as clearly as possible.

According to the ADA, a person has a disability if he or she has "a physical or mental impairment that substantially limits one or more major life activities ... a history or a record of such an impairment, or ... is perceived by others as having such an impairment."

In other words, people are protected by the ADA if they have a condition affecting their body or

mind that would greatly limit their ability to perform activities such as breathing, walking, talking,
hearing, seeing, learning, concentrating, sleep-
ing, caring for themselves, doing tasks with their
hands, or working. They are also protected if part
of their body has trouble functioning, like their
immune system, digestive system, brain, lungs,
or heart.

The second part of the ADA's definition—the part
that mentions "a history or record of ... an impairment"—says people are also protected if they used
to have a disability but do not have one anymore.
For example, if a job applicant had a serious illness in the past and is now cured, but she is turned
down for the job because the company is afraid the
illness will return and limit her ability to work, this
person is protected by the ADA.

The last part of the ADA's definition protects
individuals who are treated unfairly because other
people—like teachers or bosses—believe that they
have a disability that limits their life functions,
even if they do not. For instance, a person who has
many scars on his body might not have any differences in ability at all, but he is protected by the
ADA if his boss thinks of him as having a disability, believes he is less qualified to perform his job
duties, and treats him unfairly as a result.

Even though the ADA specifies that a condition
must substantially limit a life activity, that does not
mean that a person's disability must be severe in
order for her to be protected by the law. For example, with few or no exceptions, a person with mild
autism or mild cerebral palsy would still be covered.

Although this teenager with diabetes uses an insulin pump to control her symptoms, she is still considered to have a disability and is covered under the ADA.

Do Adaptations Count?

Many people with disabilities use tools or coping strategies to help them adapt, but when determining whether a person has a disability, these tools must not be considered. The ADA uses a fancy term to refer to these adaptations: "mitigating measures." Mitigating measures include medication, mobility devices, hearing aids, and low-vision devices (except for ordinary eyeglasses or contact lenses). For example, imagine that a student has diabetes, but it is well controlled with medication. He is still considered to have a disability (and is therefore protected by the ADA) if his diabetes would significantly impact his life activities without that medication. The only exception to this "mitigating measures" rule relates to ordinary glasses and contacts. If a person with eyesight issues can achieve full vision with glasses or contacts, she might not qualify as a person with a disability.

Myths & Facts

Myth: There are not many students with disabilities.

Fact: According to the National Center for Education Statistics, 13 percent of all public school students ages three to twenty-one received special education services in the 2014 to 2015 school year.

Myth: Private schools do not have to follow ADA laws.

Fact: Most private schools do have to follow ADA laws, but religious institutions, like churches, temples, and mosques are exempt from the ADA. However, if religious schools receive money from the government, they must follow the ADA.

Myth: If two students have the same disability, they will benefit from the same accommodations.

Fact: Even two students with the same disability might require different accommodations to reach their full potential. But it's a good idea to research the types of accommodations that have helped others with the same disability to get some ideas of what might be useful.

Chapter Two

Knowledge Is Power: Your Rights in the Classroom

Students with disabilities can face a variety of challenges in school. Maybe they have trouble taking tests, memorizing material, or concentrating. Maybe they struggle to navigate the hallways or carry a heavy backpack. Whatever their challenges, they should know that they are not alone. There are many students like them, and there are three main laws in place to help them reach their full potential in the classroom: Section 504 of the Rehabilitation Act of 1973, the Americans with Disabilities Act (ADA), and the Individuals with Disabilities Education Act (IDEA).

Understanding the Law

Those first two laws—Section 504 and the ADA—apply to every student with a disability. Section 504 says that a student cannot be discriminated against in a program or activity that receives money from the government, including public schools. This law allows any student with a disability that impacts a major life function to receive a 504 plan, which will help him receive the accommodations he needs to succeed within a regular general education classroom.

The ADA differs from Section 504 because the ADA states that discrimination against students with disabilities is not allowed in any government program, activity, or service, even if that program, activity, or service does not receive money from the government.

That IDEA law applies to students who need special education services because of their disabilities. These students are protected under IDEA in addition to Section 504, which means that they are entitled to an Individualized Education Program (IEP): a detailed document unique to one person that outlines specific goals and accommodations for the school year. With an IEP, students may be placed in a special education classroom when needed or provided services in a general education classroom.

An IEP provides all of the benefits of a 504 plan—so if a student is given an IEP, she will not have a 504 plan—but IEPs have some additional protections that 504 plans do not. One of the most useful protections included in an IEP is something called prior written notice. Prior written notice means that the school is required to notify parents in writing before any changes are made to a student's IEP. The school must also provide prior written notice if it refuses to grant a request for changes to an IEP. Remember this rule because prior written notice can act as an incredibly powerful tool. If a student or her parents make a request that is denied or put off until a later date, they should ask for a prior written notice form.

When students or parents ask for prior written notice, it is more difficult for the IEP team to simply say no. They must explain why they refused, and sometimes—if they are unable to come up with good-enough reasons—they will change their mind and grant the request. But even if they do not change their mind, prior written notice will ensure that the issue has been documented and will be

 ## What Kinds of Accommodations Might Be Helpful?

Accommodations (also referred to as "reasonable accommodations," especially in conversations about the ADA) are changes or adjustments that help a person with a disability achieve success and equal opportunity in school, the workplace, and the community. All students with disabilities are entitled to accommodations as part of their IEP or 504 plan, but the types of accommodations that are helpful will depend on each student's disability and individual needs.

Students with mobility-related disabilities might want to ask for a locker at the end of a row so that they can access it more easily and have more space for stability in case they start to lose their balance. They might also request an extra set of textbooks to be kept at school so that they don't need to carry heavy books back and forth, and they might need to switch classrooms if a meeting place is in an inaccessible location.

Those with attention-deficit hyperactivity disorder (ADHD) or learning disabilities might require testing in a separate, quiet room to minimize distractions so they can perform at their best, and they might need extra time on those tests because of focusing issues. To get the most out of lessons, it might also be helpful to ask for a copy of class notes or get permission to create digital recordings of lectures.

Students with visual impairments may benefit from digital lecture recordings, too, and they might also ask for access to Braille versions of text or large-print books. A seating location close to the board may be helpful as well.

Accommodations such as Braille textbooks can help students with visual impairments reach their full potential.

discussed again. If the school makes changes to an IEP or denies a request without providing prior written notice, it is violating the law.

Many schools also provide prior written notice before changes are made to 504 plans. However, they are not required to do that. While prior written notice is required for IEPs, schools need to provide only prior verbal notice before making changes or denying requests for students who have 504 plans.

Adding or Adjusting Accommodations

Remember that there's no pressure to anticipate all of the accommodations that will be needed throughout a school year. Sometimes it's difficult to know that an accommodation is required until a difficult situation comes up, and that's OK. It is completely reasonable to say, "I didn't realize that this would be difficult until now, and I need help."

Also, if an accommodation has been provided, but it's not as helpful as it needs to be, let a teacher or a parent know so that it can be adjusted. For example, perhaps a student has been given a separate, quiet room for testing. If she finds that she is still distracted while taking her tests because this room is right next to a noisy hallway, then she can—and should—make sure that the situation is addressed. Maybe the teacher can arrange for her to take tests during less busy times of day when there's less traffic in the hall or in another, quieter room.

Heading Off to College

All public and private colleges and universities are required by the ADA to be accessible to students with disabilities. Colleges and universities must make accommodations unless those accommodations would cause an "undue hardship" (meaning that they would be very difficult or expensive to put in place) or would fundamentally change a service, activity, or program.

If a college denies an accommodation, it needs to work with the student to find alternative

Many college students with learning disabilities receive tutoring services as an accommodation. A tutor can help a student excel in his classwork so he can reach his full potential.

accommodations. For example, if a student asks for an exemption from a required math course because of a learning disability, and his college decides that this exemption would change its program too much, it can deny this request and come up with other solutions. Perhaps the student could receive tutoring services to help him master the material. Or, if he has trouble performing calculations quickly, he could receive extra time on the quizzes and tests. There are often many paths to success.

Tackling Standardized Tests

Some students with disabilities may qualify for accommodations on standardized tests like the SAT or ACT. A school staff member such as a special education teacher or guidance counselor can submit a request for those accommodations. If the student already receives the requested accommodations through his IEP or 504 plan, and if he uses the accommodations in regular school testing, then the request will probably be approved quickly and easily.

There are many different accommodations that a student could receive, but they often include extended time, extra breaks, or longer breaks. Be careful, though! Students who have been approved to receive accommodations on college entrance exams should make sure that they understand exactly what they have been given. For example, a student with dyslexia should be aware that she may receive extended time on reading comprehension parts of the test, but not for other sections such as mathematics. A student with severe anxiety or ADHD might be eligible for extended time on every section.

Deciding to Disclose

Students must decide if they will disclose their disabilities to colleges. Some applicants feel that their disabilities help explain aspects of their applications that admissions officers might otherwise find concerning, such as a lower grade or standardized test score. Others may decide to emphasize their disabilities as a strength in their admissions essays. They might explain how their challenges have helped them develop perseverance and adaptability, for example, and their story could help distinguish them from other applicants in a positive way.

But students who worry that their disabilities might set them apart in a negative way should know that applications are not allowed to ask if students have disabilities or a history of disability. Applicants should feel free to mention their disabilities as additional information, but they should not feel obligated. And while students with disabilities can be rejected from a college due to factors such as low grades and test scores (just like any other student), the ADA protects them from being denied just because they have a disability.

But does a student have to disclose that she has a disability after she is accepted to college? Yes, she must register with the college's disability office, but only if she requires accommodations. The disability office will work with her to create an official list of accommodations that she has been approved for, and she will receive this list in an envelope. She is then expected to give this envelope to her professors to inform them about the accommodations she requires. She does not have to tell her professors about her specific diagnosis, and the disability office must keep that information confidential.

If a student does not feel comfortable going into specifics about her disability, that's OK. She doesn't owe anyone an explanation and shouldn't feel pressured to reveal private information—but she shouldn't simply hand her professors a list of accommodations and leave. If she decides she doesn't want to share her diagnosis, she should figure out ahead of time how she will frame her condition when she gives her envelope to her professors. For example, instead of saying, "I have cerebral palsy," if that's not something she is comfortable sharing, she could say, "I have some trouble getting around." Similarly, if she has dyslexia, she could say, "Sometimes I have trouble processing what I'm reading," or, "I have trouble with reading comprehension."

But if she is comfortable being open about her disability, that can work to her advantage. Not every professor is understanding and helpful, of course, but most of them tend to be appreciative when students are clear about their needs. The list of accommodations provided by the disability office is often vague in order to protect privacy, so if students can share more specific information beyond what is included on that list, professors will have a clearer idea of how to help, and students can avoid misunderstandings later in the semester.

Reaching Out

Once a student has been accepted to a college, he should reach out to the disability services office as soon as possible. Even though every college must follow the ADA, some schools are more welcoming and accommodating to students with disabilities than others.

Exploring the disability section of a college or university website and visiting the disability services office in person, if possible, can help students determine if a school will give them the support they need. When they decide on a college, they will need to submit documentation providing evidence of their disability. The source of this documentation depends on the type of disability. For example, a general practitioner or neurologist might provide a letter for someone with cerebral palsy while a psychiatrist or psychologist will provide documentation for someone with bipolar disorder. To prove

Specialists can provide documentation for students with disabilities who need accommodations in college. A young adult who is deaf or hard of hearing might consult an audiologist for this documentation.

a learning disability, colleges often request the results of a recent academic achievement test for a learning disability. The disability services office of a particular school can tell students exactly what they need to submit.

Lastly, here's a note for students who are worried about paying for college: if a student can only attend part time because of her disability, the ADA and Section 504 allow modifications to be made so that she can still take out a student loan, even if that loan would otherwise require full-time attendance.

IEPs, 504s, and Accommodations in Higher Education

IEPs and 504 plans do not transfer to college, but that's no reason to panic. Students can still receive many of the same accommodations they were entitled to in high school. In fact, colleges usually refer to a student's high school accommodations to figure out what will be needed in college. And campus life is different from high school, so sometimes students need new accommodations, and that's OK, too!

Common accommodations include accessible housing or a single room, classrooms in accessible locations, rides to class, access to an extra set of class notes, or extra time on tests and exams. Most students know that they will need these accommodations right away. In that case, they should speak to the disability services office as soon as possible to ensure that they get the help they need. However, there's no deadline for when a student can ask for help. If he realizes that he needs assistance later on, he can register with disability services at any time.

In middle school and high school, students are not responsible for letting their teachers know about their accommodations, but higher education is different. Make sure to give your professors the list of accommodations as soon as you can. Many professors become annoyed when students wait to share their needs until a moment of desperation halfway through the semester.

Colleges and universities are required by the ADA to be accessible to individuals with disabilities. These accommodations allow students to take part in the full college experience.

Mentioning the need for accommodations before there's a problem equals less stress for both the student and professor.

The ADA is there for students at every stage of their educational journeys. From the early years to university, the law gives them the right to the tools they need to succeed every step of the way.

Chapter Three

On the Job: Your Rights in the Workplace

Whether you are looking for a job now or planning your future career, it's important to remember that students with disabilities can be—and currently are—successful, contributing members of the workforce. People with disabilities are our teachers and lawyers, our doctors and nurses, and our postal workers as well as writers, artists, filmmakers, mechanics, engineers, salespeople, cashiers, and chefs. And the Americans with Disabilities Act (ADA) is in place to help them excel.

What Does It Mean to Be Qualified?

According to the ADA, it is against the law for an employer with fifteen or more employees to discriminate against a qualified person with a disability.

Notice that the ADA protects only those employees who are qualified for a position. There are two parts to the definition of this word.

People who are qualified have the required skills, experiences, and education to apply for a particular job. For example, disability or not, a

Accommodations such as screen magnification software or optical character recognition, which speaks printed text aloud, help office professionals succeed at work.

person cannot expect to be hired as a medical doctor if he does not have a medical degree. Similarly, if an employer requires applicants to have five years of experience in a certain field and a person with a disability is rejected because she only has one year of experience, the employer would not be violating the ADA.

In addition, people who are qualified must be able to perform the "essential functions" of a job, with or without reasonable accommodations. Once again, notice that there are two parts to this definition: essential functions and reasonable accommodations.

Whether a job duty counts as essential is determined by considering several factors, including the employer's opinions about what is essential, job descriptions, the amount of time that is spent performing that function, what would happen if the person did not perform that function, and the work experience of other individuals with that position.

In the workplace, reasonable accommodations are changes or adjustments to a job or the work environment that allow a qualified individual with a disability to have the same opportunities and privileges as somebody without a disability or enable that person to perform the essential functions of the job. The possibilities for reasonable accommodations are endless. An accommodation might mean providing a sign language interpreter for someone who is deaf or hard of hearing, modifying an office to make it physically accessible for a person who uses a wheelchair, or changing a work schedule.

Reasonable accommodations must be provided unless they are found to be an "undue hardship," which means that they require "significant difficulty

Reasonable accommodations can take many forms such as providing a sign language interpreter for an employee who is deaf or hard of hearing.

29

or expense." Except for very small companies, expense is rarely found to be an undue hardship. If an accommodation is found to be an undue hardship, the employer must look for alternative options to accommodate the employee.

To obtain accommodations, employees just need to ask, but it's often a good idea to get the conversation down in writing so that both the employer and the employee clearly understand what is being requested and what is being provided.

Accommodations Q&A: Know Your Rights

Am I entitled to accommodations if I work at a church?

Yes. Religious institutions, like churches, temples, and mosques, do not have to follow the ADA for members of the public, but they do have to follow the ADA for their employees.

Do break rooms have to be accessible?

Yes. Every part of the office that is available to other employees, even nonwork areas such as break rooms, cafeterias, kitchens, and restrooms, must be accessible unless this would create an undue hardship. Work-related events outside of the office, like conferences and parties, also need to be accessible.

Is it more difficult to be fired as a person with a disability?

No. An employer cannot fire somebody just because that person has a disability, but after required accommodations have been provided, people with disabilities are held to the same performance standards as any other worker.

Should I Tell?

Job applicants and employees with disabilities often wonder if they should disclose their conditions. That can be a difficult decision, and, ultimately, it depends on the situation and the applicant's preferences. Applicants often avoid mentioning a disability in a cover letter unless the position is disability related and having a personal experience with a disability would be an advantage. Many people—especially those with invisible disabilities such as diabetes, Asperger's syndrome, or depression—also avoid disclosing this information during the application process due to the stereotypes and prejudices that society often associates with disabilities. Requests for accommodations can be made at any time during the process of applying or during employment.

However, especially in a face-to-face interview, people with visible disabilities might decide that

An employee prints a t-shirt design created by a teenager with Asperger's syndrome. Sometimes employees choose not to tell employers about their disabilities, especially if their condition isn't an obvious one.

it is best to acknowledge their conditions early to minimize awkwardness and address any concerns an employer might have. Remember: the ADA says that no job applicant or employee is required to disclose his or her disability unless a reasonable accommodation is needed.

If accommodations are needed, the applicant or employee will need to disclose both his disability and the accommodation he is requesting. The employer must keep this information private. If an employee has multiple disabilities but needs accommodations only for one of his conditions, he needs to mention only the disability that relates to the accommodations.

Job-Seeking with a Disability

Many teenagers and young adults struggle to find jobs, but this process is often more challenging for people with disabilities. However, a lot of organizations and programs are devoted to helping job seekers with disabilities find jobs. One example is ABILITY Jobs (www.abilityjobs.org), which is an employment website that allows people with disabilities to anonymously submit their résumés for potential employers to review. These sites often offer résumé-writing advice and interview tips as well.

Job seekers who aren't sure where to begin might find it helpful to create a list of their skills, interests, and experiences, including volunteer work, and use that list to create their first résumé. Don't be discouraged if that résumé is short; everyone has to start somewhere!

How Do I Tell?

When mentioning a disability, always frame it in a positive way. Emphasize characteristics that your disability has helped you develop that would come in handy in the workplace, such as tenacity, adaptability, and compassion. In fact, when disclosing a disability during an interview, some applicants choose to use a common interview question, such as "What are your strengths?" as an opportunity to mention a disability. Just be sure not to dwell on limitations.

If this is an uncomfortable topic for you to discuss—as it is for many people with disabilities—practice talking aloud with a trusted friend or family member, or even alone, until the words flow more naturally. Developing and rehearsing a script, which is a specific plan of what to say, can help people with disabilities feel more at ease when the issue comes up.

Employers are not allowed to ask job applicants any disability-related questions or require them to undergo medical exams, but they are allowed to ask applicants to explain or demonstrate how they would carry out specific job-related tasks.

After an applicant has received a job offer, employers are only allowed to ask disability-related questions or require medical exams if all new employees are required to answer these questions or undergo these exams. And once a person with a disability becomes an employee, medical questions or a medical exam are typically allowed only if employers need documentation of a disability to provide accommodations or if there is concern that a medical condition would prevent an employee from safely or effectively performing a job. In all cases, employers must keep their employees' medical information private.

Medical Leave

For short-term issues or less serious health problems, regular paid sick leave—absences that

Tips and Tricks Outside of the ADA

Accommodations don't have to be official to be helpful. Sometimes small, informal changes can help employees with disabilities be more successful in the workplace, especially for people who might be uncomfortable disclosing their condition to an employer. For example, a person with attention-deficit hyperactivity disorder (ADHD) who has a desk job might use a fidget spinner (or a more discreet alternative) to help her stay focused. Or maybe all employees in a company are given the option to work from home, not just those with disabilities. A person with a disability who has trouble commuting or who requires a more flexible work schedule could pursue this arrangement without requesting formal accommodations under the ADA.

companies allow all employees to take when necessary—is usually enough. In some cases, though, employees with long-term medical issues require longer absences than their sick days allow. The Family and Medical Leave Act (FMLA) entitles eligible employees up to twelve weeks of unpaid leave each year if they need to take care of a serious health condition, but this law may not apply to small companies or to employees who are new or part time. However, even if employees don't qualify for leave under FMLA, they may be able to receive medical leave as a reasonable accommodation under the ADA. After medical leave has been granted, a full- or part-time employee with a disability is permitted to return to the same job unless keeping that position open would create undue hardship for the company. Before that employee returns to work, however, an employer can ask disability-related questions or require a medical exam if he believes that the employee will not be able to perform essential job functions anymore or will be a health or safety risk.

Above all, remember that the ADA is there to help applicants and employees with disabilities reach their full potential. Successful employment is not an undertaking that needs to be handled alone; the law is there to help.

Chapter Four

Beyond Work and School

L ife isn't just about work and school and neither is the Americans with Disabilities Act (ADA). The ADA protects people with disabilities outside of the classroom and workplace, too, whether they are at the grocery store, using public transportation, eating out at a restaurant, or catching a movie at a theater.

Places that offer goods or services to the public must be as accessible as possible under the ADA. Business owners are required to remove or update any structures that would prevent accessibility, as long as this process wouldn't cause them undue hardship or significant expense. However, keep in mind that a hardship for one business might not be a hardship for another! For example, a chain restaurant would be required to make more accessibility changes than a small, family-owned restaurant because the larger company would have more money and resources available. In practice, this means that larger businesses tend to be more accessible than smaller, local businesses, although that's not always the case.

In addition, the ADA prohibits these public places from discriminating against people with disabilities, which means that they are not allowed to turn somebody away or provide unequal treatment based on a disability. For example, it would be illegal for a barbershop to refuse service to somebody with autism simply because of that person's disability.

Heading to the Theater

Just like any business open to the public, movie theaters are required to be physically accessible for wheelchair users and others with mobility-related disabilities. However, as of 2016, theaters must also have closed-captioning equipment and assistive listening devices available for deaf or hard of hearing customers. There must be trained staff members available to help with this equipment if needed.

A group of families watch a sensory-friendly performance of *The Lion King* at the Boston Opera House. Sensory-friendly productions make going to the theater more enjoyable for people on the autism spectrum.

Many theaters and live performance venues offer sensory-friendly performances, even though this accommodation isn't required under the ADA. In these showings, the theater adjusts the lights and sounds to fit the needs of moviegoers with autism and similar disabilities, and the rules are often relaxed to allow customers to get up from their seats and move around.

Accessibility: There's an App for That

Here's the bad news, which comes as no surprise to most people with disabilities: even with the ADA in place, businesses are often inaccessible. Now for the good news: technology is helping to change that! One example of such technology is AccessNow, an app that was developed by a woman with muscular dystrophy who envisioned a more accessible future. Via the AccessNow website or mobile app, people can share information about the accessibility of specific stores and businesses by placing a green pin where buildings are accessible and a red pin where they aren't. The power of AccessNow is twofold: it helps people with disabilities plan their trips, and it raises awareness of the widespread accessibility issues throughout the United States and around the world.

Check out http://accessnow .me to search for a spe cific location, explore the map, or contribute information about a building's accessibility.

Maayan Ziv, a disability advocate who lives with muscular dystrophy, created the AccessNow app to help fulfill her vision of a more accessible world.

Planes, Trains, and Automobiles

The second section of the ADA covers public transportation systems, like public buses, trains, and subways. Under the ADA, these services must be accessible (unless, again, there is undue hardship or expense involved), and people with disabilities who use public transportation must not be discriminated against.

In addition, the ADA requires public transit agencies to provide a paratransit service for people who cannot use the regular public transportation system due to disability. Paratransit is an alternative transportation system—usually a van—that can be ridden by people with disabilities who are found to be eligible, and the system must have comparable routes and availability to the regular transit system.

Private transportation, including private buses, taxis, and airport shuttles, is covered by the ADA, too. Air travel, however, is not covered by the ADA—but don't worry! A different law, the Air Carrier Access Act, prohibits airlines from discriminating against people with disabilities. However, it's a good idea to contact the airline ahead of time if assistance will be needed. Passengers with disabilities can ask for many different accommodations. One of the most common requests is to get on the plane before other passengers (called preboarding), which can simplify a passenger's flying experience both physically and emotionally. Some airlines offer other accommodations as well, like silent boarding even before the preboarding process for individuals with autism who might need extra time to settle into

What About Service Animals?

According to the ADA National Network's website (www.adata.org), which provides resources and training on the ADA, a service animal is "any dog that is individually trained to do work or perform tasks for the benefit of an individual with a disability, including a physical, sensory, psychiatric, intellectual, or other mental disability." A service animal must be a dog or—in specific cases—a qualified miniature horse. Other species are not considered service animals under the ADA, and neither are emotional-support animals, which provide

Service animals help people with many different disabilities. This teen is visually impaired, but people with epilepsy, mobility-related issues, and other conditions use service animals.

(continued on the next page)

(continued from the previous page)

companionship and comfort to people with mental health conditions but do not have special training to perform disability-related tasks.

In general, under the ADA, service animals must be allowed in all areas where members of the public can go.

If it is unclear that an animal is a service dog, the ADA specifies that a person is only allowed to ask these two questions to make that determination:

(1) Is the dog a service animal required because of a disability?
(2) What work or task has the dog been trained to perform?

their surroundings. Certain airlines are more accommodating than others, so it's a good idea to check out the different options before booking a flight.

Reservations: Ticket Sales and Hotel Rooms

Headed to a concert or a baseball game? Under the ADA, venues are not allowed to charge higher prices for accessible seats than they charge for non-accessible seats in the same seating area. And in general, accessible-seating tickets cannot be sold to members of the public who do not have disabilities unless the nonaccessible seats have sold out.

Similarly, accessible hotel rooms must be saved for guests with disabilities until the accessible rooms are the only ones left. When booking an accessible hotel room, however, keep in mind that "accessible" or "wheelchair friendly" can have different meanings for different hotels so be sure to ask specific questions. For example, people in wheelchairs might ask about elevator access, bed heights, light switch heights, the accessibility of the bathroom, and whether there are automatic doors. Like restaurants, large hotel chains tend to be more accessible than small hotels because they usually have more resources available and stricter policy guidelines.

So whether they are headed out to eat at a restaurant, hopping on a city bus, or booking a hotel room for their next adventure, people with disabilities should be aware that the ADA protects their rights to equal access. And when places in the community aren't accessible, simply mentioning that barrier to access can help create positive change.

When booking a hotel room, people with mobility-related disabilities may want to ask specific questions about the bed, shower, and other features to make sure they are all accessible.

10 Great Questions to Ask a Business Owner

1. Is there accessible parking near the entrance of the store?

2. Is the building entrance accessible to someone who uses a wheelchair, walker, crutches, or a cane?

3. Is the entrance wide enough for a wheelchair to get through?

4. Are there Braille menus or large-print menus available?

5. Are the aisles wide enough for a wheelchair to get through?

6. Do the restrooms have enough space to be accessible to a person in a wheelchair?

7. Are there tables at an appropriate height for a person in a wheelchair?

8. Does the restaurant have options for customers with food allergies or sensitivities? What steps are taken to avoid cross-contamination?

9. How are the noise levels, lighting, and crowds? Are there certain times of day that are less busy?

10. Is the entire business accessible to a person with a disability, or are only certain areas accessible? If only certain areas are accessible, which areas are not?

Chapter Five

How to Get Help

Standing up for one's rights doesn't necessarily mean going to court and suing someone. It might simply mean speaking to a teacher or a boss when something isn't accessible. Unfortunately, violations of the Americans with Disabilities Act (ADA) are pretty common, and the government does not perform ADA inspections to make sure that existing businesses, schools, and workplaces follow the law, so it's up to the public to report any violations.

In most cases, people without disabilities do not realize they are violating the ADA because they aren't familiar with the specifics of the law or how to interpret it. Their ignorance doesn't mean that they are excused from breaking the law—they aren't—but it does mean that resolving the issue might be easier than it first appears. Before taking any further steps, make sure that your concerns don't stem from a simple misunderstanding.

And remember: people who stand up for their rights aren't burdens, and they shouldn't feel guilty for speaking up when there is a violation of the ADA. They should feel proud, because they are helping the world become more open and inclusive.

By asserting their rights, they are working toward a better future not only for themselves but also for other people with disabilities.

What to Do When Your Rights Have Been Violated

If you feel that you're not getting the support you need, first try to resolve any conflicts in an informal manner. If a violation is occurring at school, speak to a teacher, guidance counselor, or principal, depending on the situation and who makes you feel most comfortable. It is a good idea to have a parent or another trusted adult with you.

If the violation is work related or at a business or other public place, consider approaching a manager or the human-resources department. Make sure there isn't a misunderstanding; if a reasonable accommodation is required but is not being granted, clearly state the accommodation that is needed and explain why it is necessary. As much as possible, get this communication in writing. Keep records of what was said, and be sure to save those records, because they will come in handy if further action is needed.

In many cases, informally approaching someone about an issue you're having is enough to reach a solution. But what if that tactic doesn't work? In that case, it might be time to submit a formal complaint. Keep in mind, though, that the government requires formal complaints be submitted within six months of the incident in order to be considered. When pursuing this option, it's also important to remember that

If teens with disabilities feel like they aren't receiving the accommodations they need, it's often a good idea to discuss those concerns with a teacher, guidance counselor, manager, or another trusted adult.

it can take a long time for complaints to be reviewed and for incidents to be resolved. This option isn't a quick fix at all, and it can be emotionally difficult, so be sure to consider all your choices carefully before deciding to move ahead. And in all legal matters, be sure to talk to an expert, such as a disability lawyer.

For employment-related issues, submit an inquiry to the US Equal Employment Opportunity Commission (EEOC). The EEOC allows people to begin the process online, in-person at an EEOC office, or by mail.

For violations of the ADA that are not employment related, submit an inquiry to the U.S. Department of Justice (DOJ). If that sounds daunting, don't worry!

It's pretty simple to get started; just submit an online form. Mail and fax are also options, although letters and packages sent via the postal system will be delayed for security reasons, so the online form is likely the fastest method. Accommodations can also be made for people who cannot submit via the online form, mail, or fax.

Often, after reviewing a complaint, the DOJ will encourage both sides to resolve an issue through mediation. Mediation is a free, informal way of

How to Speak Up About Accessibility

There's no doubt about it: it's frustrating to encounter a public place, school, or work-place that isn't ADA accessible. Bringing the issue to someone's attention—mentioning it to a teacher, business owner, or manager, for example—is often the best first step, but speaking up can be hard. Here are some tips to make it an easier experience:

- Try to stay calm. It's completely under-standable to be upset when something is inaccessible, but people will be more likely to listen (and the conversation will probably be more productive) if the situation is approached without anger.

- Provide specific information about what needs to be changed. "Your store is not accessible" is less likely to create change than a specific request, such as: "Your store has stairs leading up to the entrance, so as a wheelchair user, I'm not able to come inside. Would you be able to install a ramp to allow people with disabilities to visit?"
- Mentioning the law can help, too. Some businesses, schools, and workplaces aren't as familiar as they should be with the ADA.
- If talking to a business owner, mention how the change would benefit the business as well. Although businesses should want to become more accessible simply because it's the right thing to do, they might be more motivated to make changes if they understand that accessibility could mean more customers and greater profits.

solving a problem with the help of a trained person—a mediator—who does not pick favorites in the dispute. The mediator simply helps both sides work together to assist them in reaching a solution that they both agree upon. Nobody is forced to participate in mediation, but it often works well. And it is less expensive and time consuming than a legal battle, so it may be a good option to try.

Looking for a Lawyer

Although many accessibility issues can be resolved informally, sometimes legal action is necessary. After the EEOC or DOJ have processed a complaint, it may be time to seek a lawyer's help. Here are some tips to keep in mind during the search:

- For the sake of convenience, try to pick a lawyer that lives in a nearby location.
- Make sure the lawyer has dealt with disability-related cases before, and ask about the outcomes of those past cases. If similar past cases were successful, that's a positive sign!
- Ask about the expected outcome of the case. The lawyer won't be able to give a guarantee, but it's a good idea to establish expectations.
- Ask about the expected fees and expenses. Hiring a lawyer can be expensive, so it's important to be aware of the costs from the start to avoid any surprises.

You Are Not Alone

There's no doubt about it: encountering accessibility obstacles is hard. Many accessibility issues will not require any sort of legal process to fix, but it can still be intimidating to approach teachers, bosses, business owners, and other community members to point out barriers to access or bring attention to discrimination. But remember: this challenge does not have to be dealt with alone.

Forming connections and finding a support network can sometimes be tricky for teens with disabilities, but there are lots of different avenues that can provide a sense of community. Reach out to family members and friends for support, or approach a trusted teacher or guidance counselor. Consider joining school groups that sound fulfilling or exciting, as extracurricular activities can be a great way to find friends with similar interests. And other people who also have disabilities can be a fantastic resource because they might have first-hand experience with similar issues. Sometimes it's most helpful to talk to the people who "get it."

Many teens with disabilities find that social media helps them connect with others who have the same issues they do. A quick search will reveal Facebook groups for people with just about any condition, and these communities can be an awesome resource for support, encouragement, and information. Just be sure to stay safe while online, watch out for cyberbullying (and tell a trusted adult if this happens!), and check the privacy of the group because anybody can see what has been posted on a page that has been set to public.

People who wish to become even more involved in the disability community often decide to engage in disability advocacy, which means that they speak or write publicly about disability rights. Advocacy is an awesome way to make a difference and form friendships with other people who have disabilities.

Connecting with others who have disabilities is a great way to find support, understanding, and encouragement. Remember: you are not alone.

But above all, advocate or not, don't be ashamed about speaking up. Every time somebody with a disability speaks up for his rights, he is paving the way to a more accessible world for every person with a disability.

Be proud. Be confident. Be a trailblazer for a better, brighter future. People with disabilities are no stranger to challenges, but within every challenge is an incredible opportunity for change.

Glossary

accessible Able to be used by people with disabilities so that they can receive the same benefits or opportunities as people without disabilities.

accommodate To provide changes that allow equal access and equal opportunity for a person with a disability.

disability A physical or mental condition that significantly limits a major life activity.

disability advocacy Speaking or writing publicly about disability rights.

discrimination Unfair or unequal treatment.

Equal Employment Opportunity Commission (EEOC) A government agency that helps people get equal treatment and opportunities in the workplace.

essential function A job duty that an employee must be able to do, with or without reasonable accommodations.

504 plan A plan created to ensure that a student with a disability receives the accommodations needed to succeed in school.

Individualized Education Program (IEP) A plan that puts in writing that students with disabilities have a right to special education services and other accommodations that they need to succeed in school.

Individuals with Disabilities Education Act (IDEA) A law that guarantees children with disabilities between ages three and twenty-one (or until high school graduation) the right to a free public education that will give them access to the services they need.

invisible disability A disability that is not easily noticed by other people. Invisible disabilities can include autism spectrum disorder, learning disabilities, and mental health disorders. Also called a hidden disability.

mediation A usually less expensive way of solving a legal problem or argument with the help of a trained person called a mediator. The mediator helps both sides work together to find a solution they both find fair. ADA mediation through the Department of Justice is free for both parties.

mitigating measure A tool or coping strategy that a person might use to adapt to her disability, such as medication, hearing aids, or crutches.

paratransit A transportation service, like a van, that can give rides to people with disabilities who are unable to use the regular transportation system.

preboard To allow a person with a disability to get on an airplane before other passengers.

prior written notice A rule that says the school must notify parents in writing before changes are made to a student's IEP or if the school refuses a request for changes to an IEP.

reasonable accommodation A change or adjustment that helps a person with a disability achieve success and equal opportunity in school, the workplace, and the community.

service animal A dog (or, sometimes, miniature horse) that has been trained to perform tasks to help a person with a disability.

For More Information

ADA National Network
(800) 949-4232
Website: http://www.adata.org
Facebook: @adanetwork
Twitter: @ADANational
The ADA National Network provides extensive
  information and guidance about how to use the
  ADA to improve the quality of life for individu-
  als with disabilities.

Broad Futures
2013 H Street NW, 5th Floor
Washington, DC 20006
(202) 521-4304
Website: http://www.broadfutures.org
Facebook: @broadfutures
Instagram: @broadfuturesdc
Twitter: @BroadFutures
Broad Futures helps young adults with learning
  disabilities achieve employment success through
  mentoring and transitional work experiences.

Council of Canadians with Disabilities (CCD)
909-294 Portage Avenue
Winnipeg, MB R3C 0B9
Canada
(204) 947-0303
Website: http://www.ccdonline.ca
Email: ccd@ccdonline.ca
Facebook: @CouncilofCDNS
Twitter: @ccdonline

CCD aims to help people with disabilities with issues relating to employment, access to services, and transportation accessibility, among other issues. Giving people with disabilities a greater chance to participate improves the accessibility and inclusivity of Canada for the benefit of all people with disabilities.

Disability Rights Advocates (DRA)
2001 Center Street, Fourth Floor
Berkeley, CA 94704-1204
(510) 665-8644
Website: http://www.dralegal.org
Email: frontdesk@dralegal.org
Facebook and Twitter: @dralegal
DRA is dedicated to protecting the legal rights of people with disabilities. It has offices in both California and New York and defends people with disabilities whose rights have been violated.

Disability Rights Education & Defense Fund (DREDF)
3075 Adeline Street, Suite 210
Berkeley, CA 94703
(510) 644-2555
Website: http://www.dredf.org
Email: info@dredf.org
Facebook: @DREDF.org
Twitter: @DREDF
DREDF is a law and policy organization that works to protect and advance the rights of people with disabilities.

DisAbled Women's Network Canada (DAWN)
469 Jean Talon W., #215
Montréal, QC H3N 1R4
Canada
(514) 396-0009
Website: http://www.dawncanada.net
Facebook: @DawnRafhCanada
Twitter: @DAWNRAFHCANADA
DAWN Canada works to help women with disabilities who struggle with poverty, isolation, violence, or discrimination.

Incight
111 SW Columbia Street, Suite 1170
Portland, OR 97201
(971) 244-0305
Website: http://www.incight.org
Facebook, Instagram, and Twitter: @Incight
Incight's goal is to eliminate the stigma surrounding disability and to help people with disabilities find employment and educational opportunities.

National Disability Rights Network (NDRN)
820 1st Street NE, Suite 740
Washington, DC 20002
(202) 408-9514
Website: http://www.ndrn.org
Facebook and Twitter: @NDRNadvocates
The NDRN serves as the membership organization for programs that provide legal services to people with disabilities.

For Further Reading

Anner, Zach. *If at Birth You Don't Succeed: My Adventures with Disaster and Destiny.* New York, NY: St. Martin's Griffin, 2016.

Burdick, Debra. *Mindfulness for Teens with ADHD: A Skill-Building Workbook to Help You Focus and Succeed.* Oakland, CA: New Harbinger Publications, 2017.

Landau, Jennifer, ed. *Teens Talk About Learning Disabilities and Differences.* New York, NY: Rosen Publishing, 2018.

Oslund, Christy. *Succeeding as a Student in the STEM Fields with an Invisible Disability: A College Handbook for Science, Technology, Engineering, and Math Students with Autism, ADD, Affective Disorders, or Learning Difficulties.* Philadelphia, PA: Jessica Kingsley Publishers, 2013.

Paddock, Bonner. *One More Step: My Story of Living with Cerebral Palsy, Climbing Kilimanjaro, and Surviving the Hardest Race on Earth.* New York, NY: HarperCollins, 2015.

Schab, Lisa M. *The Self-Esteem Workbook for Teens: Activities to Help You Build Confidence and Achieve Your Goals.* Oakland, CA: New Harbinger Publications, 2013.

Shea, Therese. *ADD and ADHD.* New York, NY: Rosen Publishing, 2014.

Shusterman, Neal. *Challenger Deep.* New York, NY: HarperTeen, 2015.

Steigler, A. J. *When My Heart Joins the Thousand.* New York, NY: Harper Teen, 2018.

Bibliography

AccessNow. "Our Mission." Accessed February 18, 2018. http://accessnow.me/about.

ADA.gov. "Introduction to the ADA." Retrieved January 4, 2018. https://www.ada.gov/ada_intro.htm.

ADA.gov. "Movie Captioning and Audio Description Final Rule." Retrieved February 15, 2018 .https://www.ada.gov/regs2016/movie _captioning_rule_page.html.

ADA National Network. "What Are a Public or Private College-University's Responsibilities to Students with Disabilities?" Retrieved January 11, 2018. https://adata.org/faq/what-are-public -or-private-college-universitys-responsibilities -students-disabilities.

Brennan, Jacquie. *The ADA National Network DISABILITY LAW Handbook*. ADA National Network. Retrieved January 11, 2018. https://adata.org /publication/disability-law-handbook.

Darling, Nancy. "Disability? In College? Advice on Talking to Professors." *Psychology Today*, June 12, 2015. https://www.psychologytoday.com /blog/thinking-about-kids/201506 /disability-in-college-advice-talking-professors.

FindLaw. "Transportation and the Americans with Disabilities Act (ADA): Q&A." Retrieved February 15, 2018. http://civilrights.findlaw.com /discrimination/transportation-and-the -americans-with-disabilities-act-ada.html.

Goldin, Tal M. *Student Rights: A Handbook to the Educational Rights of Students with Disabilities in Montana*. Disability Rights Montana. Retrieved February 15, 2018. http://disabilityrightsmt.org /janda3/files/home/Buttons/2016.08 .31%20Student%20Rights%20Handbook.pdf.

Institute of Education Sciences National Center for Education Statistics. "Children and Youth with Disabilities." Accessed February 1, 2018. https:// nces.ed.gov/programs/coe/indicator_cgg.asp.

Martin, Jeff. "Prior Written Notice Is a Powerful Tool When Skillfully Used." Wrightslaw, January 22, 2016. http://www.wrightslaw.com/info/pwn .refusal.martin.htm.

Samuels, Christina. "What Does Federal Law Say about Vouchers and Students with Disabilities?" Education Week June 7, 2017. http://blogs .edweek.org/edweek/speced/2017/06/federal _law_and_students_with_disabilities.html.

Seigel, Thomas. "12 Questions to Ask Your Potential Lawyer." Lawyers.com. Accessed February 1, 2018. https://www.lawyers.com/legal-info /research/12-questions-to-ask-your-potential -lawyer.html.

Texas School for the Blind and Visually Impaired. "Possible Accommodations for the Student with a Visual Impairment." Retrieved January 7, 2018. http://www.tsbvi.edu/instructional-resources/3657 -vision-accommodations.

US Department of Education. "Protecting Students with Disabilities." Accessed January 7, 2018. https://www2.ed.gov/about/offices/list/ocr /504faq.html.

US Department of Justice. "ADA Mediation Program." September 2016. https://www.ada.gov/mediation_docs/mediation-program.htm.

US Department of Justice. "Ticket Sales." Retrieved February 15, 2018. https://www.ada.gov/ticketing_2010.htm.

US Department of Labor. "Office of Federal Contract Compliance Programs (OFCCP)." Retrieved January 4, 2018. https://www.dol.gov/ofccp/regs/compliance/faqs/ADAfaqs.htm.

US Equal Employment Opportunity Commission. "The ADA: Your Responsibilities as an Employer." Retrieved January 9, 2018. https://www.eeoc.gov/eeoc/publications/ada17.cfm.

US Equal Employment Opportunity Commission. "Pre-Employment Inquiries and Medical Questions & Examinations." Retrieved January 7, 2018. https://www.eeoc.gov/laws/practices/inquiries_medical.cfm.

Wright, Peter, and Pamela Wright. "Key Differences Between Section 504, the ADA, and the IDEA." Wrightslaw, January 31, 2017. http://www.wrightslaw.com/info/sec504.summ.rights.htm.

Index

A

accessibility, 5, 37, 39, 42–43, 48–51

accommodation, 34–35, 48
 adding, or adjusting, 16, 18, 29, 37
 public, 4, 9, 7–13, 37–44
 reasonable, 8, 16, 28–29, 32, 36, 46
 school, 14–26
 undue hardship, 19–20, 29–32, 36–37, 40

Americans with Disabilities Act (ADA)
 defined, 4–6
 five titles, 8–9
 national network web-site, 41
 public access, 37–44, 46, 48
 rights in school, 14–26
 rights in the workplace, 27–36
 specifics of the law, 7–13
 violation of rights, 45–52

anxiety, and depression, 4, 21, 31

attention-deficit hyperac-tivity disorder (ADHD), 17, 21, 35

autism, 4, 11, 38, 40

B

Braille, 17, 44

business, 5, 9, 37–39, 44–46, 48–50

C

cerebral palsy, 11, 22–23

college and university
 disability services office, 22–25
 disclosing a disability, 21–23
 IEPs, 504s, and accommo-dation, 25–26
 public and private, 19–20
 student loan, 24
 testing, 20–22, 24–25

D

deaf/hard of hearing, 9, 29, 38

diabetes, 12, 31

disability
 advocacy, 51–52
 invisible, or hidden, 4, 31
 and learning, 11, 17, 20, 22–24
 mobility-related, 12, 16, 37–38
 rights, 14–26, 27–36, 45–52

discrimination, 4–5, 8, 14–15, 27, 37–38, 40, 51

dyslexia, 4, 21–22

F

formal complaint, 46–47, 50

About the Author

Kerry Elizabeth Benson received her undergraduate degree from Connecticut College, where she studied neuroscience. She is now pursuing a graduate degree in science writing at Johns Hopkins University. Benson, who has mild cerebral palsy, works as a tutor for high school students and is passionate about helping people with disabilities reach their full potential.

Photo Credits

Cover FatCamera/E+/Getty Images; p. 5 kali9/E+/Getty Images; p. 7 Fotosearch/Archive Photos/Getty Images; p. 9 ZUMA Press Inc/Alamy Stock Photo; p. 10 BSIP/Universal Images Group/Getty Images; p. 12 Photographee.eu/Shutterstock.com; p. 17 Andrew Aitchison/Corbis Historical/Getty Images; p. 19 Monkey Business Images/Shutterstock.com; p. 24 monkeybusinessimages/iStock/Thinkstock; p. 26 Andersen Ross/Blend Images/Getty Images; p. 28 Valery Sharifulin/TASS/Getty Images; pp. 29, 52 Lokibaho/E+/Getty Images; p 32 Michal Cizek/AFP/Getty Images; p. 38 Boston Globe/Getty Images; p. 39 Andrew Lahodynskyj/Toronto Star/Getty Images; p. 41 Wang He/Getty Images; p. 43 Education Images/Universal Images Group/Getty Images; p. 47 Fstop123/E+/Getty Images.

Design: Tahara Anderson; Editor: Jennifer Landau; Photo Researcher: Sherri Jackson